on foot

walks and
quizzes

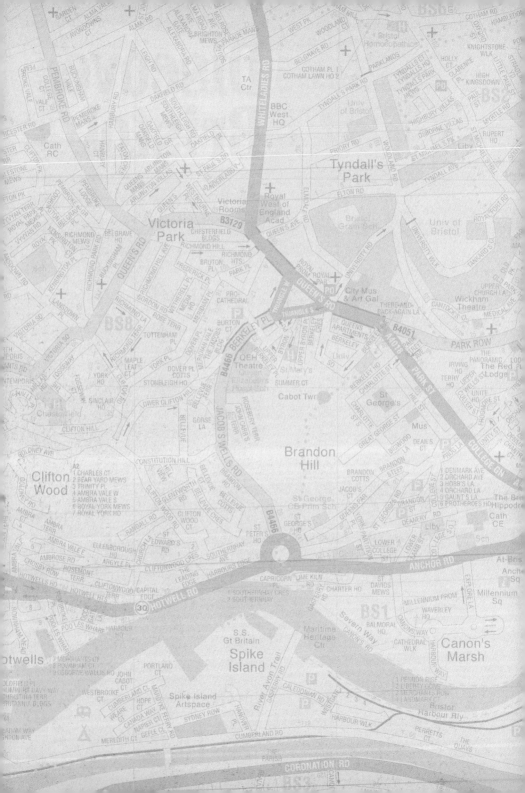

Discover Bristol on foot

walks and quizzes

John Dennis & Robin Haward

redcliffe

First published in 2008 by Redcliffe Press Ltd.,
81G Pembroke Road, Bristol BS8 3EA

www.redcliffepress.co.uk
info@redcliffepress.co.uk

ISBN 978-1-904537-90-8

British Library Cataloguing-in-Publication Data
A catalogue record for this book is available from the British Library

Design and typesetting by E&P Design
Printed by HSW Print, Tonypandy

Contents

BEETLING AROUND BRISTOL

All walks start at Nicola Hicks' beetle sculpture in Anchor Square, Harbourside. Allow 1–1½ hours for each walk.

The rhinoceros beetle is, size for size, the world's strongest creature. It can lift up to 850 times its own weight.

Acknowledgements

We love Bristol and we've loved writing these quiz walks. We hope you find great enjoyment in doing them and that they will encourage you to look at parts of Bristol in a slightly different way.

There are many people we'd like to thank. Without the constant badgering of Michelle Bond and Gemma Rigby we would never have got the walks written… we could simply have enjoyed coffee indoors in the dry. Thank you.

We would like to give enormous thanks to our band of walk checkers, especially the two to whom we are married – Mariasol Dennis, a patient help with the technology, and Angela Haward, who has been an assiduous checker; to Paula Whiting, Sarah Scott, Hilary Perry and Nick Parsons.

We would also like to thank Bob Bell, not only for brilliant photographs but also for major amounts of enthusiasm.

Thanks must also go to Tim Davey of the *Bristol Evening Post* for publishing four of the walks in *Seven* magazine.

Lastly we are very grateful to our publishers, John, Angela and Clara Sansom of Redcliffe Press, for believing in the project.

DISCLAIMER

The face of Bristol is changing all the time. Whilst we have made every effort to ensure accuracy, the writers and publishers cannot accept any responsibility for changes which may have occurred in the Bristol cityscape nor for the safety of walkers. Please take care.

Walk 1
Redcliffe

Start at the beetle sculpture at Harbourside and head towards the water and over the bridge (known as Pero's Bridge, built to commemorate the slave owned by John Pinney, the Bristol plantation owner). Walk up Farr's Lane and cross into Queen Square. Walk with the square on your left.

▶ *What used to be situated at number 37?*
▶ *Who used to live two doors along?*

2

Cross to the statue, one of the finest equestrian statues in the country.

▶ *Who is the man on the horse?*
▶ *When was the statue first erected?*

Find Queen Square House. On its front wall you will see four statues.

▶ *What is represented by the statue on the right?*

From Queen Square House, turn left and leave the square with the equestrian statue on your left. At the junction with King Street you will see two pubs.

▶ *When was the Llandoger Trow built?*
▶ *How did it get its name?*

The pub on the other corner is a famous jazz pub, The Old Duke. There are several theories about its original name, The Duke's Head. Was it named after the Duke of Cumberland or the Duke of Wellington?

Duke Ellington, the American jazz musician, is on the pub sign now.

The Old Duke

Turn right past the Llandoger Trow towards the water, then right again. On the corner with Little King Street is an ornate building. It used to be a grain warehouse.

▶ *How many different forms of arches can you count?*

Continue along Welsh Back. At the end of the street you will see a pub, The Hole in the Wall, which has a spyhole facing the water. This is where sailors would go to look out for the press gangs roaming along The Grove. Any sailor 'pressed' might well find himself an unwilling member of a crew crossing the Atlantic!

Who is the man on the horse?

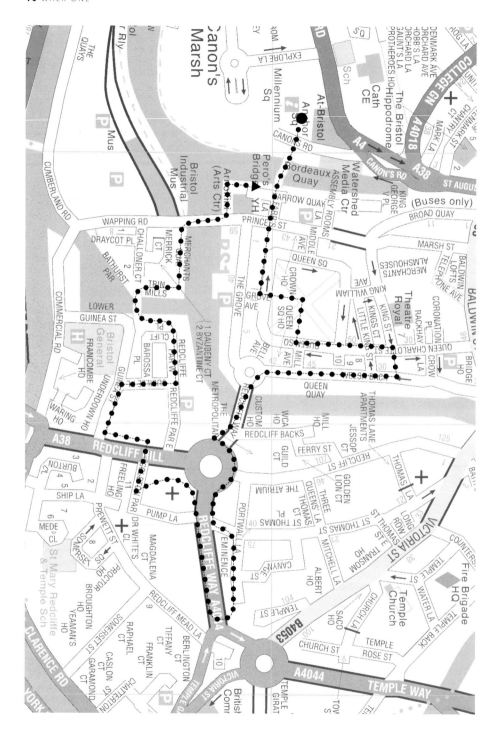

It is also, almost certainly, the pub used by R L Stevenson as the place where Jim Hawkins first met Long John Silver in *Treasure Island* (see walk 8, St Michael's Hill). Look at the sign of the pub.

▶ *How many pillars support the first storey of the pub?*

Turn left, cross the bridge and continue towards the church of St Mary Redcliffe. At the pedestrian crossing cross to the right-hand side of the road and continue to the Quakers' Burial Ground.

▶ *Who now owns the burial ground?*

Return via the crossing to the left side of the road and continue until you arrive at a statue of a phoenix.

▶ *How many flames surround the phoenix?*

Continue down Portwall Lane to Phippen Street and then right. In front of you is Chatterton's house.

▶ *Who built Chatterton House?*
▶ *How old was Thomas Chatterton when he died?*

THE LLANDOGER TROW

An interesting pub built in about 1664 as five houses. FIVE? If you look at the gables you can see three: a further two were destroyed by bombing in the Second World War. It is worth looking at as it's a good example of timber-framed construction.

Many people think (wrongly, we're sorry to say) that Robert Louis Stevenson came to this pub to gather 'atmosphere' for his famous *Treasure Island* and it's also said that Daniel Defoe met with Alexander Selkirk, the 'real' Robinson Crusoe, here. Selkirk had survived alone on a desert island and had then been picked up and returned to England.

Where did the Llandoger Trow get its name? Well, a trow is a large flat-bottomed sailing barge. These barges used to trade across the river Severn from nearby Welsh Back. Llandoger comes from Llandogo, the name of the village on the river Wye which joins the Severn near the first Severn crossing, now the M48.

Retrace your steps and and head towards the beautiful church of St Mary Redcliffe. On a visit to Bristol Queen Elizabeth I pronounced it the 'fairest, goodliest, most famous parish church in England' – and she saw it without its magnificent spire!

If the church is open, enter.

▶ *What is remarkable about the North Porch icon?*

Inside the church turn to the right to see a huge whale bone.

▶ *Who gave it to the church?*

Move towards the south door. Study the wrought-iron screen by the door.

▶ *What animal can you find represented in the screen?*

Leave the church by the south door. Turn left and look for a small gravestone in the grass. It has an unusual inscription.

▶ *What is the inscription?*

Walk towards Fry's House of Mercy and the railings.

▶ *What appeared in the churchyard on Good Friday 1941?*

Leave the churchyard by the gate (top right-hand corner) to Redcliffe Hill.

Note: if the church is not accessible, go into the churchyard via the Redcliffe Hill gate. If you are really unlucky and the churchyard is locked too, walk along the road by the railings.

Turn left up Redcliffe Hill to the pedestrian crossing at the lights and cross to Guinea Street. Numbers 10–12 were originally one house belonging to Edmund Saunders, a captain of a slave ship who sailed 20 slaving voyages. He was also the warden of St Mary Redcliffe church.

▶ *What is the date of the house?*
▶ *What is the carving above the right window of number 11?*

Turn right along Alfred Place and Jubilee Place and stop for a moment in the car park in Redcliffe Parade to admire the view. See if you can pick out a shot tower, Bristol Bridge, Cabot Tower and Ashton Court Estate.

Make your way down the ramp. You can see where Redcliffe gets its name.

Continue along the wharf.

▶ *Why might the wharf you are standing on have been named Alfred Wharf?*
▶ *For what was the sand excavated from the red cliffs used?*

Continue past The Ostrich pub. This dates from at least 1745.

▶ *How many windows does the pub have? Include doorlights.*

Cross the swing bridge, turn right then left and walk along Merchants Quay. At the end turn right and cross the next swing bridge. You will see the Arnolfini, one of Europe's leading centres for the contemporary arts. Cross the road and walk down with the building on your right, and find the statue of John Cabot.

▶ *When did Cabot sail for North America?*
▶ *Who created the statue?*

Walk to the main entrance of Arnolfini.

▶ *When was the complex created?*

Continue to the Youth Hostel.

▶ *What type of staircase is visible in the building?*

Continue to Pero's Bridge. Before you cross, find a plaque.

▶ *Where was Pero born?*

Over the bridge and back to the beetle ●

PERO

Pero Jones was the personal servant of John Pinney, a plantation owner on the island of Nevis in the Caribbean. At the age of 12 he was sold to Pinney, along with his sisters, Nancy and Sheeba and one adult slave for £115. He was luckier than most black slaves working for white masters; he was spared the cruel and exhausting life of a field slave and brought to England to live and work as a servant at 7 Great George Street, just off Park Street (now the Georgian House Museum).

Pero returned home to Nevis with the Pinneys twice, once in 1790 and 1794. Four years later, in 1798, he became ill. John Pinney was concerned about his health, and sent him to live in Ashton. He died that same year.

Very few black slaves actually came to Bristol; most were transported from the Guinea coast of Africa (there is a Guinea Street near St Mary Redcliffe) to the plantations of the Caribbean and the southern states of America.

The footbridge across the River Frome in the harbour, built in 1999, is named after him.

Walk 2
Brandon
Hill Park

Start at the beetle and walk towards the Explore building and exit the square on the right. At the main road, turn left. On your left you will see a cone sculpture.

▶ *What is the name of the sculpture?*
▶ *Who does it commemorate?*

Continue along the road until you come to the next controlled crossing, signposted Bristol Cathedral. Turn left and enter College Square on the right. Walk up to the Norman Gatehouse arch of the old abbey, now Bristol Cathedral. Ahead of you is an imposing statue.

▶ *Who is the gentleman?*

Walk away from the Cathedral, following the statue's gaze, and turn right down College Street. Cross to Brunel House via a small car park and pedestrian crossing. Bear right and look through an arch if you want to see the sculpture of Horse and Man which commemorates the site of the nineteenth-century Bristol horse market. Otherwise go left up Brandon Steep to Brunel House. On the corner of Brunel House find the plaque.

▶ *What was it built as originally and what was its name?*
▶ *Who were based at 2 Brandon Steep?*

Bristol Cathedral

Who is this gentleman?

4

Take the path into Brandon Hill Park, the right fork, following the wall. At the gate turn left. You will have the adventure playground on your left, and views of the warehouses down in the city. You will come to a junction of the paths, with a sign board.

▶ *What did the old Police Station become?*

5

Continue over the intersecting path past the tree commemorating Richard Norris. Then right again, up steps, pausing to take in views of Dundry and the Somerset hills. Turn right then left, with the pond and water features on your right.

▶ *When was the oak tree planted?*
▶ *To celebrate what event?*

6

Make your way to the tower.

▶ *In what year of Queen Victoria's reign was the tower erected?*
▶ *What were the names of John Cabot's three sons?*
▶ *When was the foundation stone laid?*

7

Climb the tower, if open.

▶ *How many steps did you climb?*

Replica of the city cross of Bristol

8

Admire the views of Bristol, the great tower of the Wills Memorial Building of Bristol University and Isambard Kingdom Brunel's ship the ss *Great Britain*. Catch a glimpse also of the Clifton Suspension Bridge over the river Avon.

▶ *How many miles are you from Land's End?*
▶ *And John o'Groats?*

9

Leave the tower and go straight ahead. After about 40 metres you will pass a seat given in memory of Leah Robbins. Continue until you reach a T-junction by public toilets. Turn left, and continue with a pond on your left.

▶ *What other cities join Bristol as a Peace Blossom site?*

10

Keep going down the path, past the exit to Charlotte Street, then after about 40 metres turn right into Berkeley Square. Walk down the square with the gardens on your left. You will see a replica of the city cross of Bristol (the original is in the gardens of Stourhead, in Wiltshire). At the bottom of the square, turn left.

▶ *Who used to live at number 23?*

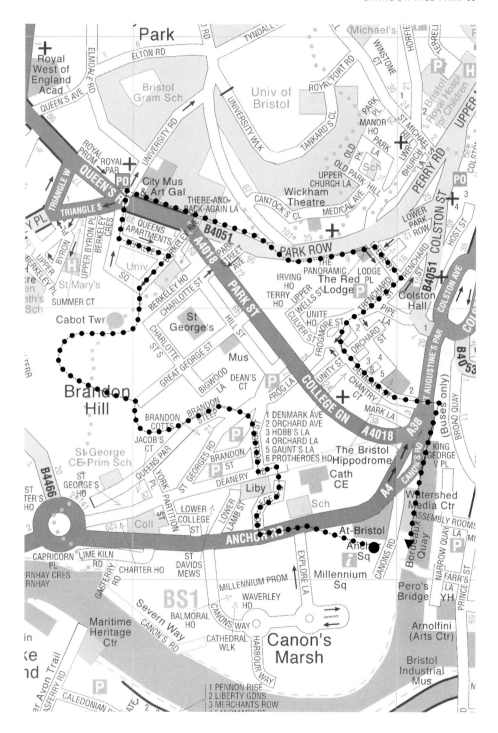

JOHN CABOT

That John Cabot climbed out of his boat somewhere on the coast of North America on 24 June, Midsummer's Day, 1497 is not in doubt, nor is the fact that he never returned from a second voyage the following year.

What else do we know?

He was born Giovanni Caboto (caboto is the Italian word for 'coasting seaman') around 1450, probably in Genoa. We do know that he became a citizen of Venice in 1476 and to qualify for that status he must have lived there for 15 years. He came to England in the 1490s and in 1496 was granted Letters Patent from King Henry VII, which gave him permission to make his transatlantic voyage.

Accompanying him on the voyage was one of his sons, Sebastian, who later became a famous seaman in his own right. It would have been useful if he had spent some time recording his father's achievements! They sailed on a single boat, *The Matthew*, possibly the anglicised name of Mattea, Mrs Cabot.

Though Cabot's voyage is the most celebrated one, sailors from Bristol had been sailing west to try to find the Isle of Brasile and the Isle of the Seven Cities since the 1470s, the most well-known being in 1480 led by Bristolian John Jay.

Incidentally, the collector of customs in Bristol at the time, and the man responsible for the finances of the voyage, was called Richard Ameryk.

At the end, turn right. At the pedestrian lights cross over to the Venetian-looking building which used to house the Bristol Museum. Turn right and walk towards the present day museum and art gallery. Notice the plaque.

▶ *What does it commemorate?*
▶ *When did it happen?*
▶ *How many years later was his famous American relative born?*

Follow the road along into Park Row for about 200 metres. Don't go down Park Street. Notice the statue above the white door.

▶ *What has the building just before Woodland Road to do with HMV records?*

Cross to the other side of Park Row, and continue left.

If you have time and it is open, visit The Red Lodge, Bristol's beautiful Tudor house. Don't forget to see the Knot Garden. All plants grown here are known to have been growing at the time of Red Lodge being built.

▶ *When was Red Lodge built?*
▶ *What is its connection with Lady Byron?*

Turn right down Lodge Street. At the bottom turn right along Trenchard Street. Then fork left by Bristol's oldest pub, The Hatchet. There are two dates on the pub, c.1500 when it was established, and another when it was first licensed.

▶ *When was The Hatchet first licensed?*

Go left down Denmark Avenue, which becomes Denmark Street, to the main street, St Augustine's Parade.

Turn left and cross at the lights. Notice the imposing statue of Neptune, one of the centre's popular landmarks.

▶ *When was Neptune 'born'?*
▶ *Where was his first 'home'?*

Continue towards the water, with the fountains on your left and find a plaque in memory of Samuel Plimsoll.

▶ *Where was Samuel Plimsoll born?*

![17]

Continue and walk alongside the Floating Harbour, past the bars, restaurants and Watershed Media Centre until, on your right, you meet up with the beetle ●

SAMUEL PLIMSOLL

Many a sailor's wife will have been grateful to Samuel Plimsoll, born in Bristol in 1824. Why? It's all to do with ships. When you own a ship the temptation used to be to put as much on it as possible, to make more profit. This was bad news as ships tended to be overloaded. Result? In a heavy sea or a storm they were more likely to sink, with the needless loss of sailors' lives. Samuel Plimsoll changed all this.

He was responsible for the Merchant Shipping Act of 1876 which made it law that merchant ships had to be inspected and had to have a line painted on them to show the safe loading limit. As more and more goods were put on the ship it would sit lower and lower in the water until the painted line was reached by the water level. Then, stop! No more loading… and a much safer voyage. This brilliant safety idea quickly came to be known as the Plimsoll Line and Plimsoll himself became known as the 'Sailor's Friend'.

Walk 3
Broad
Street

1

Leave the beetle and head for Pero's bridge. Cross it and then turn left immediately. Continue to the 'waterfall' steps, then, using the pedestrian crossing, move on to Broad Quay. Walk along, crossing Baldwin Street, until you come to St Stephen's Avenue. Walk down it a few yards and you will notice a plaque in memory of James Fuller Eberle.

▶ *What was erected in his memory?*
▶ *By whom?*

2

Continue along what has now become Colston Avenue until you see a building with shields on its front. This is Quay Head House, built as the Bristol Municipal Charities Office.

▶ *How many shields are displayed along its front?*

3

Continue straight on into Quay Street and past the old city gate to St John's Conduit on the right.

▶ *Where is the source of this water supply?*

4

Retrace your steps for about 35 metres and enter the old city by St John's Gateway. Queen Elizabeth I entered Bristol through this very gate in 1574. Once through, look back at the figures of Belinus and Brennus, the legendary founders of the city.

▶ *What are the two figures holding?*

St John's Gateway

Shell porch at Tailors' Court (see overleaf)

The Seven Stars (see overleaf)

Walk up Broad Street and notice the former Everard Printing Works building on the left.

▶ **Which century is mentioned in the tiles on the left?**

On your right you will come to the Guildhall.

▶ **Which courts are held at the Guildhall?**

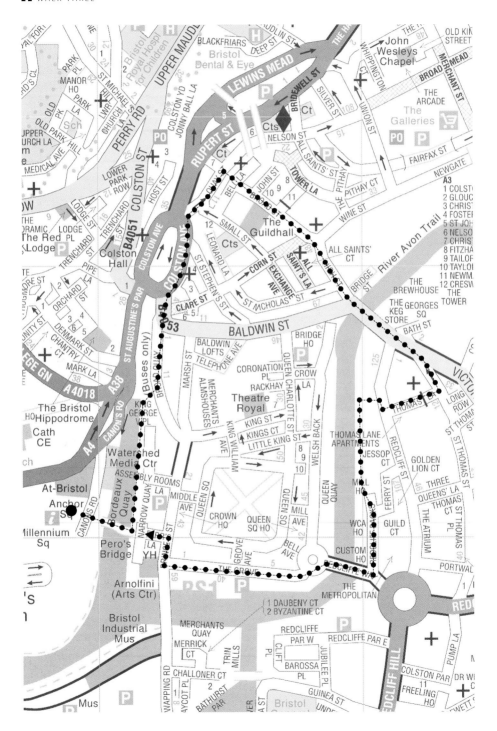

7

Immediately opposite the Guildhall you will see a small passageway to Tailors' Court. Walk through, looking at the iron edges to the pavement which were there to stop the carriage wheels damaging the stonework. When you are in Tailors' Court study the decorated porch on your left.

▶ *Who was the gentleman whose head is on the plate?*

8

Continue to the end of the court and look at the Court House on your right.

▶ *What is the date of the Court House?*

9

Return to Broad Street. Continue to the end where it reaches Wine Street. Notice the clock of Christchurch with its quarterjacks.

▶ *What colour are their boots?*

10

Go down High Street to, then over, Bristol Bridge. Continue to cross Redcliffe Street, then bear right down St Thomas Street. Notice a row of town houses. They were built 1673–75 but there were shops on the site way before that.

▶ *When were the shops there?*

Christchurch quarterjack

11

Turn right at the redundant church of St Thomas the Martyr, down Thomas Lane, to The Seven Stars.

▶ *Who stayed at the inn in 1787?*
▶ *What was his purpose?*

BRENNUS AND BELINUS

These two brothers were the legendary founders of Bristol.

The story goes that, in prehistoric times, England was ruled by King Malmutius. It is said that when he died, the country was divided into two, with his two sons sharing the kingdom; Brennus was given the area in the north and Belinus that in the south.

Brennus was not a happy man. He had all the mountainous wild parts whilst his brother got the nice parts (like Bristol). The two were all set to go to war with each other until their mother stepped in and said they should share the kingdom equally. That's what mothers are for!

It is said the Romans called this area Caer Bren which means the City of Brennus.

How curious that these warmongers are shown in their statues carrying crucifixes even though they are supposed to have lived long before the birth of Christ.

Walk to the bottom of Thomas Lane, then over and slightly to the left, heading for the water.

▶ *What is the name of the obelisk?*

Down to the waterfront then turn left. Continue to the helter-skelter (blue) and, walking to the left of it, make your way up Redcliff Backs. You will be walking past the backs (landward side) of warehouses on your right. Notice the interesting building of Redcliffe Wharf.

▶ *What are the two mottoes with the plume of feathers?*

14

Turn right over the bridge and cross Welsh Back at the zebra crossing. Follow the road to The Hole in the Wall (see walk 1, Redcliffe) and round into The Grove, passing two restaurants, Severn Shed and riverstation on the other side of the road. Cross at the lights and go to the *Thekla*. This was originally a German cargo boat, which was owned at one time by Vivian Stanshall of the once famous Bonzo Dog Dooh Dah Band. Its original port of registration has been painted out but can still be read.

▶ *What was the original port of registration?*
▶ *How many anchors are visible?*

A little further along is the Mud Dock which has won awards both as an eating place and a cycle shop. Look at the side facing The Grove.

▶ *What is its postal address?*
▶ *How many steps ascend to the café?*

Look at the side facing the water.

▶ *How many pillars support the balcony?*

Continue along the waterside.

▶ *Which boat has its own post/letter box?*
▶ *What is the building next to the Mud Dock?*

At Prince Street turn right. Before you cross at the controlled crossing, look at the down pipes on the single storey brick building.

▶ *What date do you see on them?*

Cross the road to the Shakespeare, once a row of fine town houses. Study the board outside and to the left of the door.

▶ *Where does the name Prince Street come from?*

19

Turn left into Farr's Lane, cross Pero's Bridge and rejoin the beetle ●

GUILDS OR GILDS

The idea of Guilds is well established in our history. Those with a particular skill or those who traded in specialised goods would form a guild. They would get together and secure a Royal charter or a charter from a local land-owner that would give them exclusive rights over their lines of business.

So, for example, the tailors of Bristol would be members of the Merchant Tailors' Guild. They would have control over prices so that trade was fair: they would even ensure that individuals did not make grossly too much profit. In order to trade as a tailor you would have to be a member of the Guild of Tailors and abide by its rules. If you did not keep the rules you could be thrown out of the guild and then you would not be able to work as a tailor in the city.

As a member you would not be able to take part in unfair practices – for example buying up a load of cloth before the cloth market had opened. Neither would you be allowed to 'corner the market', that is buy up all the cloth so that there was none for the other tailors in the city.

Hundreds of years ago the Guildhall would have been a place of meeting for any of the guilds of the city.

Walk 4
Castle Park

1

Leave the beetle and cross Pero's Bridge. Continue into Farr's Lane and at the end turn left and walk down Prince Street. You'll pass a hotel on your left and looking across the road to your right you'll be able to see into Queen Square.

▶ *How might Middle Avenue have got its name?*

2

Continue to the road junction and look up at the building on your left.

▶ *What is represented in the first mural on the wall?*

3

Cross at the lights and enter King Street. Cross immediately to Venturers House.

▶ *What stood on this site in 1445?*

4

Walk next door to the almshouses and read the poem above the left-hand door.

▶ *What was the likely occupation of people before they retired here?*

5

Continue down King Street.

▶ *What is the date on the end wall of the almshouses, next to the coat of arms?*

THE THEATRE ROYAL

The Theatre Royal in King Street is a wonderful theatre. It was built between 1764 and 1766 to designs by Thomas Paty, who had been asked to model it on the Drury Lane Theatre in London. He made one significant change to the design, making the auditorium horseshoe shape instead of a rectangle.

The auditorium was remodelled with a new sloping ceiling and gallery in 1800 but since that date has not really changed in all that time. In the 1970s, the site was redeveloped, with modernised backstage facilities, workshops, offices and a state-of-the-art studio theatre. It also gave the theatre its magnificent entrance through the neighbouring Coopers' Hall, which dates from 1743 and was designed by William Halfpenny.

The theatre is currently (2008) closed for refurbishment.

Immediately next to this is an inscription above a door.

▶ *What is the inscription?*

Walk on past the Chinese restaurant then look across the street.

▶ *From when does the Royal Navy Volunteer date?*

Continue down King Street. Study the Theatre Royal building, the entrance to which is through the Coopers' Hall. Look carefully at the left wall of the centre doorway.

▶ *When was the Hall built?*
▶ *Who was the architect?*

Walk on down King Street to discover:

▶ *Who worked with St Nicholas in 1656?*

Cross straight over the road and walk between the two pubs and into Welsh Back and turn left. Go to the monument by the water.

▶ *To whom is this memorial dedicated?*

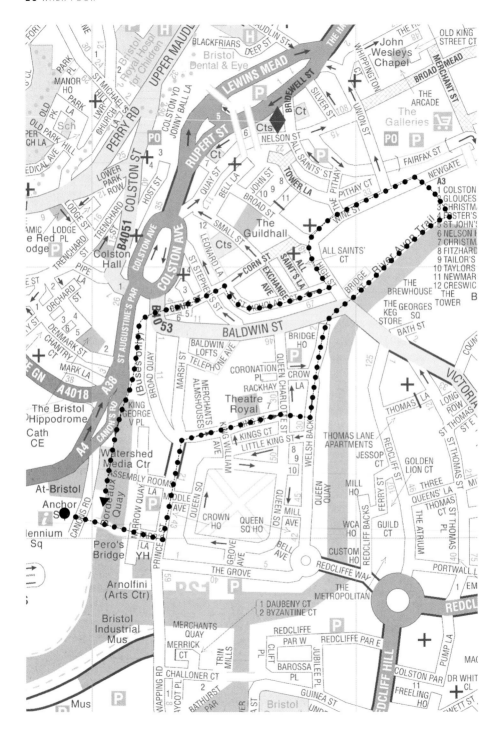

Look at the lowered quayside next to the memorial and find a plaque in the stone by the water's edge.

▶ *What destroyed the quayside next to the memorial?*

Carry on to the end of Welsh Back, passing the Brigstow Hotel on your left. Did you know that Brigstowe was an early form of the name Bristol? It means 'the settlement by the bridge'.

Look across the street at St Nicholas Church and the church clock.

▶ *What is unusual about this clock?*

Turn right and walk up to Bristol Bridge. Using the light-controlled crossing, cross into Castle Park. As you walk along the path next to the water study the red brick buildings across the water to your right.

▶ *What name is on the Bristol Brewery building?*

14

Follow this path and when you are roughly opposite the Courage Brewery, approx 100 metres from where you crossed the road, turn and study a plaque on the stone wall in the grass area to your left.

▶ *How many Bristol men died in the Spanish Civil War?*

Entrance to the sally port

Continue along the upper path by the water with the ruined St Peter's Church on your left. Find display board 9, The Barbican Gate.

▶ *How do we know that the King's Constable lived well?*
▶ *What is a 'sally port'?*

Now look to your right at a group of silver birch trees.

▶ *What is commemorated by this piece of garden?*

Continue walking straight ahead and then look left at the drinking fountain featuring two fish heads. Look carefully at the fountain as well as all the decorated bricks beneath your feet.

▶ *Who designed this fountain?*
▶ *Which school's pupils were responsible for the commemorative bricks?*

Walk down the stone slope to look at the sally port. Return to the main path and back the way you came, turning immediately right up the hill, passing the pineapple sculpture on your left. Follow the path down the hill to the road. Turn left and walk up to the next controlled crossing. Cross to the Galleries and find the plaque on the Galleries wall near the junction with Union Street.

▶ *What used to be on this site?*

Cross Union Street and keep walking along Wine Street, crossing the Pithay and continue straight ahead. Study the plaque on the wall next to the church.

▶ *Who was Bristol's Poet Laureate in 1813?*

Cross Broad Street and turn left to High Street corner.

▶ *Who lived on the corner between 1791 and 1798?*

BRISTOL CASTLE

The first castle in Bristol was built around 1068 by Geoffrey Montbray on the orders of William the Conqueror. It was a motte and bailey castle, very simple and easy to build. The motte is the Norman word for a mound. It was rather like an upside down pudding basin made of earth, very steep and impossible to run up! On top was a wooden tower or keep. A ditch was built round the perimeter to make it even more difficult to scale. The bailey was a smaller mound at the bottom, ringed by a fence where horses and cattle were kept. Bailey means an enclosed space.

The second castle was built by Robert Earl of Gloucester about 40 years later. This time the keep was built of Caen stone and stood over the great dungeon. Its great twelfth-century tower had four turrets and the foundation walls were reputedly 25 feet thick! It was one of the largest in the country at the time.

The castle was destroyed by Cromwell's forces during the civil war because it had been a royalist stronghold.

Walk down High Street, turning right into St Nicholas Street. Cross the road to St Nicholas Church and look at the plaque on the wall.

▶ *Who lived in this street?*

Continue along the street, passing St Nicholas Market. If it's open it is worth going in.

▶ *What is the building opposite the top of the steps to your left?*

23

Continue for a few metres to the Elephant pub (now, perversely called The Ivory).

▶ *Which letter can you see in the stone underneath the elephant?*

24

It is interesting that the building opposite, now a bar, is the old fish market. Walk on to number 34.

▶ *Can you see another name for this building?*

Carry on until you come to an impressive building with black marble columns. This is the old stock exchange.

▶ *What words are in stone underneath the two figures on the left of the building?*

The former stock exchange, now an Indian restaurant

Continue to the junction and then turn left into Clare Street. Walk down to number 24.

▶ *What is the date at first floor level?*

Proceed down Clare Street to the centre and cross Baldwin Street at the controlled crossing. Cross again to the centre. Leaving the fountains on your left, walk down Bordeaux Quay as far as Pero's Bridge and turn right to the beetle ●

Walk 5
The
Underfall

1

Leave the beetle, heading towards the water and Pero's Bridge. Do not cross the bridge but continue straight ahead, walking with the water to your left and the bars to your right. After about 100 metres you come to Bordeaux Quay.

Look at the Bordeaux Quay name plate.

▶ *What feature do the two crests have in common?*

2

Walk to the weather-vane tower, which is an old base for a crane.

▶ *What is written on the plate on the door?*

3

Continue along the harbourside. You are passing the Lloyds Amphitheatre building.

▶ *For what do you need the daily consent of the Harbourmaster?*

4

Walk back and around the front of the Lloyds building. Find the inscription in the middle.

▶ *What was the contribution of the City Council to the construction of the amphitheatre?*

William Tyndall

Continue round the Lloyds building and cross to the line of tall vents (from the award-winning car park beneath you).

▶ *What can you find at the base of the first vent?*

Continue into Millennium Square. Find light number 16.

▶ *Who designed the lighting?*

Find four statues at the side of the square.

▶ *Who are the people depicted in these four statues?*

Leave the square by the corner next to the silver sphere. Turn left and walk along Anchor Road, away from the city centre. Cross over the side road and continue, passing the Travelodge hotel. Stay on Anchor Road for about 450 metres, passing a roundabout on your right. As soon as you can, return to walking along the harbourside.

Note: We hope that there will be a new walkway next to the water, avoiding the need to walk by the road.

Look across the water to the ss *Great Britain*.

▶ *What is the name of the dockyard to the right of the ss* **Great Britain***?*
▶ *How many masts does the ss* **Great Britain** *have?*

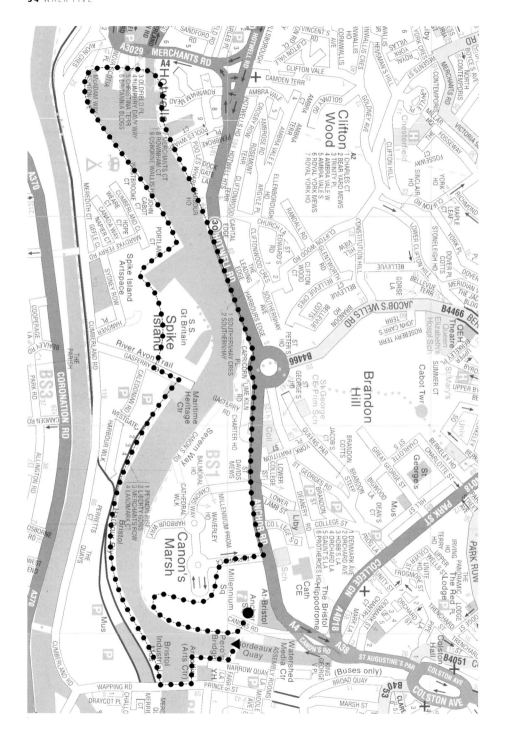

Keep walking along the dockside and find the memorial just before Poole's Wharf.

▶ *How long was the* **Flying Fox** *moored at this position?*
▶ *For what does RNVR stand?*

Carry on along the waterside.

▶ *What is the name of the marina by the footbridge?*

Continue walking until you reach the Pump House.

▶ *How many brass lamps are there on the wall of the Pump House?*

Turn left, crossing the bridge on the footway.

▶ *What is the date on the building by the end of the bridge?*

Cross the second bridge.

▶ *How many Old Dock Cottages are there opposite the Pump House?*

Turn left into Avon Crescent. After a few metres turn left through a gateway into the Underfall Yard.

Note: if these gates are locked, continue walking along Avon Crescent, join the main road and take the next turn to the left. Walk left towards the chimney of the Underfall Yard.

▶ *What is unusual, perhaps, about the chimney in the Underfall Yard?*

Look at the Underfall Yard display board by the giant tank.

▶ *Give one advantage of Ross and Sage's patent slipway.*

Continue through the Underfall Yard.

▶ *Who is the boat builder operating in the yard?*

Look around you at the boats moored by the yard.

▶ *What is the name of the Harbourmaster's boat?*
▶ *What are the Harbourmaster's office hours?*

THE FLOATING HARBOUR

Before 1809 ships entering the port of Bristol had to contend with the tides of the river Avon; with its great tidal fall, the difference between high and low tide could be as much as 13 metres. As the tide ebbed and flowed, so the boats and ships moored in the docks rose and fell with it. The ships therefore had to be very strongly built to withstand the pressure, and had to be kept upright when they were moored at low tide, to prevent the cargo from shifting inside the hold. Both these were achieved. The boats were strong and kept 'shipshape and Bristol fashion'.

However, at the start of the 19th century, the ships were getting bigger and risked being damaged as the tide fell away. Instead of coming to Bristol, ship owners were taking their trade to other ports. It was decided to divert the river and build 24-hour high water mooring facilities that allowed vessels to float between tides.

The harbour was the brainchild of William Jessop, and after years of delay the project was started in 1804. The cost was to be £200,000 (it eventually rose to £600,000). The project was supervised by his son Josias, and the digging was done by English and Irish labourers, not prisoners from the Napoleanic wars which has become a popular theory. When it was opened on 1 May 1809, the workers were treated to a feast of roast beef, potatoes and six hundredweight of plum duff washed down with an inordinate amount of strong beer which was drunk with much gusto. The outcome was a monumental brawl between the two sets of workmen, quelled by the 'Guardians of the Peace', and a lot of sore heads on the following morning.

18

Find the display board opposite the Harbourmaster's office.

▶ *When was the 'floating harbour' constructed?*

19

Continue along the harbourside, passing the Cottage Inn.

▶ *What is on the weather vanes of Brooke Court and John Cabot Court?*

20

Carry on until you come to the hand sculpture.

▶ *What is the date on the hand sculpture?*

21

Enter the marina and find the rowing club headquarters.

▶ *Complete this statement:*
  'Rowing .... for the people of Bristol'

The Fairbairn steam crane

The slipway in use

Walk around the marina.

▶ *Where would you go to get a licence to use the marina?*

Leave the marina area and follow the road round to the right. Find the red-brick building opposite the clock tower.

▶ *What is the Bristol Old Vic connection?*

THE MATTHEW

The Matthew is berthed just next to the *Great Britain* in the docks – unless she is out sailing on charter somewhere. We are talking to Rob Salvidge, Master of the *Matthew*, on board.

How often does the Matthew *have to be taken out of the water?*

Every year for survey – this is a requirement of the Maritime and Coastguard agency for all ships. We have her looked at by two maritime surveyors – including the surveyor who was involved in building her.

What are you up against with a wooden hull?

We're looking for weed and to some extent, worm. The Gribble Worm used to be common – it used to be brought back from hotter climates by wooden-hulled boats. Nowadays there's much less of it. What we are looking for is basically damage to the keel or the rudder.

So how do you treat her hull when you've got her on the slipway?

Years ago it would have been with copper-based paints… and sometimes the whole of the bottom would be covered in copper sheeting.

Hence copper-bottomed?

Yes, but now because the copper-based paint is pretty poisonous we used a basic bitumen-based paint.

How would 15th-century masters and sailors have treated the hull?

A lot of scraping and small repairs. Wood would have been 'graved' in to the damaged areas….using graving pieces and then paints with lots of animal fat.

They would have used tallow for the seams – and we still do!

How different is maintenance now compared with the 15th century?

We can choose our wood better… and there are modern glues and resins – but we try not to use them on the *Matthew*. We try to be traditional!

Is the maintenance of the hull a very expensive business?

Well, the process IS time-consuming so our labour costs are high – but the parts are cheap.

What would happen if you did **not** take it out of the water every year?

Well, we'd get a weed problem… and we'd lose our licence!

How much risk of damage is there when you are hauling her out on the slipway?

None. The slipway is very gentle. The Underfall Yard Trust restored this and it works very well.

How much would Cabot himself have known about the maintenance of his ship?

Very little! The captain was like the master of ceremonies and the real work, the real knowledge, lay with the Sailing Master. Cabot would have trusted people like Lancelot Thirkhill to look after the ship. In Nelson's time there would have been a Captain *and* a Master… and for the work to get done a Captain's mate and a Master's mate.

Keep walking along the dockside path.

▶ *Which shipbuilder uses the dry dock*
   opposite the Bristol Diving School?
▶ *What is the yellow structure across*
   the dock?

Keep walking along the path until it ends.

▶ *What offices are facing you?*

Turn left and continue down the path towards the dockside. Carry on until you reach the Maritime Heritage Centre. Find the tile work on the outside wall.

▶ *Which schools designed and made the*
   Great Tile Mural?

Continue along the dockside until you reach the *Bristol Packet* offices.

▶ *What is the name of the boat featured on*
   the buildings?

Keep walking for about 200 metres.

▶ *How many trees are there in front of*
   Brunel's Buttery?
▶ *Who built the Fairbairn steam crane?*
▶ *When did it cease to be in regular use?*
▶ *What is the name of the boat featured in*
   the Dock's mural?

Continue walking along the dockside. Study the display board.

▶ *What was the 'blood sweeten'd beverage?'*

Carry on along the dock side.

▶ *What is the name of the world's oldest*
   tugboat?
▶ *Until when did the* Pyronaut *serve in the*
   City Docks?
▶ *Who built the* John King *in 1935?*

Look at crane number 29.

▶ *How was crane 29 powered?*

Study the plaque on the warehouse roughly opposite crane 29.

▶ *What does it commemorate?*

Continue walking and turn left over the Prince Street swing bridge. Turn left by Arnolfini. Keep walking along the dockside.

▶ *What is housed in the tall redbrick*
   warehouse next to the Architecture Centre?

Continue along to Pero's Bridge. Cross the bridge and you are back at the beetle ●

Walk 6
Christmas Steps

Leave the beetle, heading towards the waterfront and turn left just in front of Pero's Bridge. Look around: you are on a covered walkway.

▶ *What are you not allowed to do on this walkway?*

Continue until you reach the Watershed. Look above the door of the Watershed.

▶ *Fill in the missing word:*
'music .... and dancing'

The buildings along here are all quayside sheds originally used for unloading and storing cargo from the ships which docked here.

▶ *Which letter of the alphabet denoted the Watershed?*

Carry on to the end of the covered way. When you're just outside, look up to your left and admire the weather vane.

▶ *What is there on top of the weather vane?*

Before you move on, look around.

▶ *What is the name of the quay along which you have just walked?*

THE WARRIOR ON THE DRAWBRIDGE

This is the figurehead of a ship. And the first thing to say is that it is a replica, but that shouldn't get in the way of a good story!

The ship, a paddle steamer, was called the *Demerara*. At 3000 tons it was the second largest ship to be built in Bristol, only the ss *Great Britain* was larger. In 1851, eight years after the ss *Great Britain* was launched, the *Demerara* was due to go to the river Clyde to have its engines fitted. This meant sailing out of the port down the river Avon with its huge tide differences and treacherous currents.

The departure was delayed and the tide had already started to ebb when they started out at a pretty brisk rate. Disaster! The ship hit rocks just beyond the unfinished Suspension Bridge, it slewed round so that its stern wedged on the opposite bank and rested on the mud as the tide went further and further out. The *Demerara* had succeeded in blocking the entrance to the port of Bristol.

Eventually it was hauled off, but it never made it to the Clyde to have those engines fitted.

Walk straight ahead until you reach the controlled crossing opposite the Hippodrome. Cross very carefully. You are outside a pub called The Drawbridge (reverting to its older name, after being called the Horn and Trumpet for a period).

▶ *What can you see standing above the clock?*

With the Drawbridge on your left, walk towards Colston Tower and cross the road by the controlled crossing at the end. Stand by the sign for Colston Street and turn and look back the way you came.

▶ *What is the date of St Augustine's Court?*

Walk up Colston Street and pause opposite the Colston Hall to admire the architecture.

▶ *How many arches are there at first floor level?*
▶ *What are the three activities shown in stone on the wall?*

Continue up Colston Street and cross Host Street, which was one of the first streets in Bristol to be paved. Look back at the old wall.

▶ *How many bricked up arches can you see in this wall?*

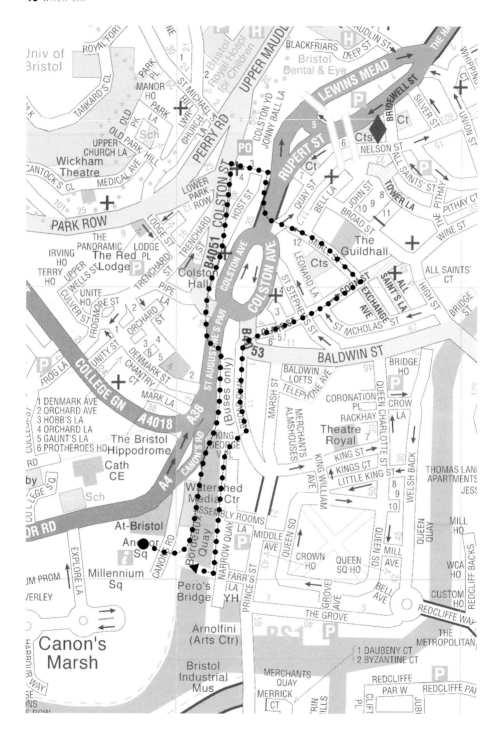

Weather-vane, Bordeaux Quay

The Drawbridge Warrior (right)
and Christmas Steps (far right)

 10

Keep going until you are opposite the junction with Lower Park Row. You are outside the gates of the former Foster's Almshouses.

▶ *When were the almshouses founded?*

 11

Look carefully at this interesting building, especially the gutters.

▶ *What figures are at the top of each down pipe? (Look behind you at the pub on the corner!)*

 12

Admire the statues of the Three Kings of Cologne, the biblical wise men.

▶ *What sort of staircase is the outside staircase?*

 13

Face up the hill again, turn immediately right and walk down Christmas Steps. Near the top are a number of niches or 'sedilia'.

▶ *Why might people have been grateful for these?*

CHRISTMAS STEPS

Climb into your time-machine and look at the steep, muddy short cut up from the banks of the River Frome to Colston Street above. Now return to the present day and admire the neat, appealing steep street of steps. Enjoy the shops, cafes and the pub. At the bottom fish and chips are served from one of the only Tudor timber-framed buildings in the city.

The steps were put in by Jonathan Blackwell at his own expense in 1669. He was Sheriff of Bristol for a time and thought up this major improvement for the citizens of Bristol. You'll notice the seats at the top for tired shoppers and if you look down the steps you will see that the street narrows – which makes the steps seem even more steep!

Christmas Steps is one of the better known parts of the city of Bristol – much photographed, painted and drawn. The steps have appeared in a film and the shops, although they change from time to time, are still endlessly fascinating. Why were they given the name 'Christmas'? Difficult to say for certain. Blackwell had a friend Richard Christmas who may have lived near or on St Michael's Hill. The steps were near Christmas Street. The name could derive from the fourteenth-century Knyfsmythe Street. Anyway – Christmas Steps – 'steppered done and finished September 1669'.

Look at the inscription near the top of the steps.

▶ *When were the steps put in?*
▶ *How many arches can you count on your right as you walk down?*

Continue down the steps admiring the shops as you go. When you reach the bottom look right.

▶ *What is the name of the pub on your right?*

Now look to your left and find a stone arch which does not seem to line up properly.

▶ *What name is just above the arch?*

From the bottom of Christmas Steps, facing the same way you came down, turn right and go under the buildings to the main road. Turn right and cross using the controlled crossing. You should arrive at the rounded end of the Royal and Sun Alliance building.

▶ *What is on the shield above the door?*

Cross the road and enter Small Street. Find number 9 and look through the outer glass door and to your left.

▶ *What can you see to your left?*

The imposing Exchange, with its clock with two minute hands

Continue up Small Street for a few metres and look up to your right. Find the plaque announcing the Civic Society Award for 1994.

▶ *What is this building?*

Retrace your steps for a short distance and cross to the double-porched building. Find the plaque.

▶ *When was John Foster the Lord Mayor?*

Continue up the street to the impressive building set back from the road.

▶ *What is this building?*

Continue to the top of Small Street and into Corn Street and look at the wonderful Exchange slightly to your left. Look at the clock, it has two minute hands – the red one shows original 'Bristol' time – a reminder when Bristol, 120 miles to the west of London, was literally minutes behind the capital city.

▶ *What is the time difference?*

Notice the fine Bristol 'nails' along the front of the Exchange. It is said that these nails, where Bristol merchants used to pay and receive money, are the source of the expression 'paying on the nail'. Study the nail nearest Small Street.

▶ *What is the inscription around the edge of the top flat surface?*

Go down Corn Street towards the centre. Look at the Commercial Rooms on your right and the frieze or relief above the door.

▶ *Besides people, what can you see depicted in this frieze?*

Continue down Corn Street and look left at the Old Bank. Look carefully at the tops of the ground-floor windows.

▶ *What has the central head got which the others have not?*

Keep going down Corn Street and cross over St Stephen's Street.

You are now in Clare Street. Continue and cross St Stephen's Avenue. At the bottom use the controlled crossing to cross Baldwin Street to your left. You should find yourself on Broad Quay. Walk down it to the controlled crossing and cross, heading for the arched brick feature. Look above the lion.

▶ *In whose memory is this feature constructed?*

Look round the other side of the lion and find two figures.

▶ *What do the figures represent?*

Continue along the quayside. Look left through railings into a courtyard of offices. You will see a sculpture of Sabrina, Goddess of the River Severn.

▶ *How many figures are there in the sculpture?*

Staying on the quayside, head towards Pero's Bridge. Look to your left at the building on the corner of Farr's Lane.

▶ *What two things can you see at the top of the building?*

Cross Pero's Bridge and look very closely at the 'horns'.

▶ *What might these horns be for, besides decoration?*

31

Walk straight on into Anchor Square where you rejoin the beetle ●

Walk 7 Lewins Mead

1

Leave the beetle and walk towards the horned bridge. Don't cross but turn left, walk to the end of the covered walkway. Cross St Augustine's Parade at the second pedestrian crossing, near the Hippodrome. Turn right and cross Colston Street. You will come to a church with six Corinthian columns. This whole area was once on the waterfront.

▶ *What clue to this can we gain from the name on the church?*

2

A play, *The Winslow Boy*, written just after the Second World War by Terence Rattigan and made into a film with Nigel Hawthorne in 1999, told the true story of a naval cadet accused of stealing a postal order. The name of the actual cadet heads the list of those killed in the First World War.

▶ *What was the name of the cadet?*

3

Continue and walk under Centregate to Christmas Steps. Look at a pub called The Three Sugar Loaves.

▶ *What does the pub sign show?*

4

There is a gateway to one of Bristol's medieval buildings.

▶ *What is the name of the building?*

Samuel Morley

The Greyfriars stone

If the gate is open, go into the courtyard and find a display board.

▶ *When was the hospital founded?*
▶ *Which two famous Bristol schools were on this site?*

Retrace your steps to the road again and continue to the Hotel du Vin with its fine shell porch. Look at the display on the left.

▶ *What was on the site in 1728?*
▶ *How many corkscrews can you count?*

Leave Narrow Lewins Mead by the Meeting House and cross at the lights to the central reservation. There you will see a statue of Samuel Morley, the son and nephew of the Morley family who made the famous Morley nylons.

▶ *What was his connection with the city?*

Back across the road again and on to Greyfriars. There are six sculptures of St Francis of Assissi.

▶ *What scenes of his life are depicted?*

Look at the Greyfriars stone.

▶ *When was a friary built on this site?*
▶ *When was it surrendered?*

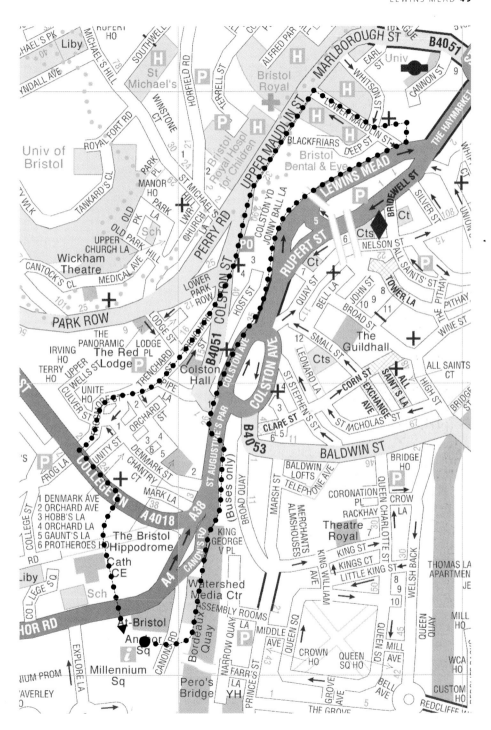

9

Follow the direction of the bus lane and cross Lower Maudlin Street and take the next turning immediately on the left under an arch with a lamp into St James' Court, the churchyard for St James' Priory, the oldest church building in Bristol. Head towards the church and, at the top, enter the churchyard by the gate on your right. Find an impressive memorial stone commemorating the deaths of the five infants of Charles Wesley, the great hymn writer. If the gates are locked you can read the inscription through the railings.

▶ *What were the names of the five Wesley infants?*

10

Exit the churchyard and bear left by the steps to find the White Hart pub on your right.

▶ *What date do you see on the gable end of the pub?*

11

Cross to the Bristol Eye Hospital. Look at the murals by the sculptor Walter Richie and the quotation.

▶ *What do we cross to from the years?*

12

Walk up the hill and turn left into Upper Maudlin Street. Continue to the Bristol Royal Hospital for Children.

▶ *How many rings are there on the Paul O'Gorman building?*

JOHN WESLEY

In 1739 John Wesley came to Bristol on the invitation of George Whitefield, a preacher who had to return to preach in America. This was all part of the Methodist Revival. John Wesley found it hard in Bristol at first – he did not like 'field preaching' (preaching out-side) – but eventually got used to it. He travelled over 200,000 miles on horseback, preaching some 40,000 sermons.

He had a great effect on his listeners in Baldwin Street and in Newgate Gaol (where The Mall Bristol is now). Numbers in the Bristol Religious Societies grew so great that a place for worship had to be built, hence Wesley's New Room in the centre of Broadmead, opened in 1741. It was the first Methodist building in the world.

All John Wesley's teaching and preaching was supported by Charles Wesley's hymns of which he wrote more than 6,000.

Wesley's New Room is open to the public and is well worth a visit.

Continue up the hill and bear left down Colston Street. When it is safe cross to the right-hand pavement. Cross Lower Park Row and down the hill. Turn right into Trenchard Street. The Griffin pub is on the corner. Continue down the hill past the back of the Colston Hall and the multi-storey carpark.

▶ *Look at the Hatchet pub. What is the date on the wall?*

Continue along Frogmore Street and climb the steps to Park Street. Turn left towards College Green to find the Lord Mayor's Chapel.

▶ *What is unique about the Lord Mayor's Chapel?*
▶ *What is its full name?*

The Lord Mayor's Chapel

Cross at the pedestrian lights and into College Green. Make your way over to the Council House, Bristol's City Hall. Look at the plaques set in the walkway.

▶ *What are the names of the five cities twinned with Bristol?*

Look at the statue of the seaman. The sculptor said it was John Cabot, but the city council insist it is an Elizabethan seaman!

▶ *What is he holding in his left hand?*

SUGAR

It is impossible to separate Bristol's sugar industry from the slave trade. Sugar was brought to Bristol from the plantations of the Caribbean as the last leg of the notorious transatlantic – or 'triangular' – slave trade.

Goods such as utensils made of brass and copper, gunpowder and firearms were loaded on to the ships here in Bristol, bound for the ports on the Guinea coast of Africa. Once arrived, these were traded for slaves who had been rounded up by African slave-traders from the surrounding regions. These were taken, in appalling conditions, on the notorious 'middle passage' to the plantations on islands such as Nevis in the West Indies. Those who survived the voyage (there was a huge amount of illness and death) would then spend their lives cutting sugar, which would then be shipped to Bristol. Bristol was the most significant English port for slave trading in the middle of the eighteenth century. In 1730 a ship left here every week.

The sugar came here to be refined – at one stage Bristol had 20 sugar refineries – and the city got rich on our love of sweet tea (see reference to Hotel du Vin on p48).

Head towards the cathedral.

▶ *What was the Cathedral formerly known as?*
▶ *Which is its oldest part?*

Take the narrow street at the east end of the cathedral, the end away from the Norman arch. Descend, looking through the double iron gates at the sculpture of the Madonna. Carry on down the steps to the bottom.

▶ *Which school has its sign by the bottom of the steps?*

Cross by the controlled crossing into Anchor Square, and meet up with the beetle ●

Walk 8
St Michael's Hill

Leave the beetle and walk towards Pero's Bridge. Do not cross but turn left and walk down the covered way of Bordeaux Quay. Continue down the Centre and cross at the pedestrian crossing opposite the Hippodrome. Turn right and cross Colston Street at the lights. Walk up Colston Street until you come to the junction with Host Street. Study the building on this junction. Notice that it won an award in 1993.

▶ *What words can you find in the ceramics which decorate the tower?*

Carry on for a few metres.

▶ *What words can you find in the ceramics in the windows of the building?*

A little further up Colston Street, cross at the zebra crossing into Lower Park Row. Begin to walk up Lower Park Row. Look across the road.

▶ *What is Zerodegrees?*

Continue up the hill for a short distance.

▶ *What is the name given to the buildings on your left?*
▶ *What date is given in the White Lodge sign on the wall?*

Sign of the old times

The Ship Inn

The old rectory

5

When you reach the Ship Inn, cross the road and at the top of the hill turn right into Perry Road. Continue down Perry Road to the traffic lights and cross. Walk left and immediately up the steps to Lower Church Lane. At the top, study the old rectory.

▶ *How many separate panes of glass go to make up each window?*

6

Continue up the steps to the right of the Old Rectory and walk to the right following the railing round. On the corner pause and look down on the building with a tower on the corner of St Michael's Hill.

▶ *Which king is featured on this building?*

7

Carry on up the hill on the raised pavement and past St Michael's church. Across the road from you there are two pubs separated by one private house.

▶ *What are the names of the two pubs?*

8

Continue up the hill and study Colston's Almshouses across the road from you.

▶ *What can you see in the small tower above the clock?*

9

Turn left into Park Place. Walk up the slope and steps and at the top turn left to descend by a very old building on your left, The Manor House, which is one of Bristol's oldest buildings, now converted into flats. Look back through the gate of The Manor House.

▶ *How many windows are set in the roof?*

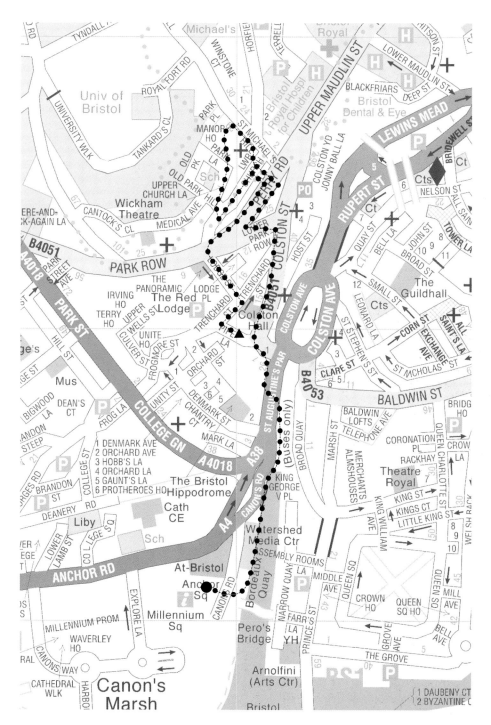

THE SCOTCHMAN AND HIS PACK

Near the bottom of St Michael's Hill you will find a pub with this intriguing name. Remember, you are outside the old city wall and standing on what used to be the main road to Gloucester. Furthermore it's a steep hill and you have a heavily laden cart drawn by a horse.

Perhaps you need to stop for refreshment, in which case you will need a scotch: a wedge to put under your wheel to stop the cart slipping back down the hill, pulling your horse with it. You'll need a man to help – a Scotchman: and his pack – the wedge he puts under your wheel. Amazing and important in those days.

Look at the brick-built hall next on your left.

▶ *What words are set in stone on the gable of the building?*

Turn right into Old Park, then left into Old Park Hill. As you descend look above the door of number 16 and you will see a sign on the wall showing three faces and a number.

▶ *What is the number on the sign?*

At the bottom turn left below the car park. You are back in Lower Church Lane. Continue along the lane. You will notice several stones set on the pavement right next to the walls of the houses.

▶ *What could be the purpose of these stones?*

Continue walking and turn right down the steps and cross at the lights to Perry Road. Turn right along Perry Road towards Red Lodge. Cross carefully and walk down Lodge Street. Cross Trenchard Street and turn right. Take a left turn into Pipe Lane. Study 6 Pipe Lane.

▶ *What is odd about the tops of the windows of number 6?*

14

Continue down Pipe Lane to Amelia Court and round the corner and back on to the centre. Walk to the controlled crossing opposite The Drawbridge and cross to the central area. Walk towards the docks. On your right you will see several stone seats with plaques.

▸ *Who presented the Bristol Basin plaque?*
▸ *Where was Cabot's son born?*
▸ *When was the Cabot Trail opened?*
▸ *When was the centenary of Bristol City's ownership of the docks?*
▸ *Which Canadian province is mentioned in the plaque nearest to the docks?*

15

Head towards the water and the covered walkway of Bordeaux Quay. At the end by Pero's Bridge turn right and rejoin the beetle ●

WOOL

In the Middle Ages the wealth of this area of the country, Wessex, was in the wool it produced. The wool was mainly the short-fibred type, needed for the fine 'broadcloth'. The length of the fibre is known as its staple.

In 1353 The Statute of the Staple named Bristol as one of the Staple ports of the country. This meant it could import and export wool to and from Europe. Good news for Bristolians. Not such good news was the arrival of Flemish weavers who came to start weaving businesses in Bristol.

One such weaver came from Flanders in 1337 and opened a thriving business. There was fierce opposition from the local merchants who claimed he did not belong to a guild. Their objections were overruled by the king, and he was allowed to continue his business.

His tomb is in St Stephen's Church, just off the city centre, and his name – Edward Blanket. No, it's not what you're thinking! The word had been in existence a hundred years before.

Quiz answers

WALK 1
REDCLIFFE

1 First American Consulate ▶ Woodes Rogers, a famous Bristol seaman and later Governor of the Bahamas
2 William III ▶ 1736
3 America
4 1664 ▶ Trows sailing from Llandogo
5 Seven
6 Four
7 Citizens of Bristol
8 12
9 Giles Malpas ▶ 18
10 Largest in any parish church since the Reformation ▶ John Cabot ▶ A mouse ▶ The Church Cat (1912–27) ▶ A tramline
11 1718 ▶ A parrot
12 King Alfred is reputed to have sheltered there ▶ Glassmaking and ballast
13 18
14 May 1497 ▶ Stephen Joyce
15 1961
16 Spiral
17 Nevis

WALK 2
BRANDON HILL PARK

1 Small Worlds ▶ Paul Dirac
2 Raja Rammohun Roy
3 Royal Western Hotel (1840–55) ▶ Bristol Savages (1907–20)
4 Avon Wildlife Trust
5 1902 ▶ Coronation of Edward VII
6 61st ▶ Sebastian, Lewis and Sanctus. ▶ 24 June 1897
7 106
8 64 miles ▶ 504 miles
9 Ottawa, Canberra, Cardiff, Edinburgh, Oslo
10 John Loudon McAdam
11 Washington's Breach ▶ 26 July 1643 ▶ 89
12 Mark Barraud, owner of Nipper, worked as scenic designer in the old Princes Theatre on this site. Nipper was the HMV dog
13 1590 ▶ She helped form a girls' reformatory here in 1854
14 1606
15 1723 ▶ Old reservoir of Temple Conduit, Temple Street
16 9 Colston Parade

WALK 3
BROAD STREET

1 A gateway ▶ The Antient Society of St Stephen's Ringers
2 23
3 Top of Park Street, then from cistern of Carmelite convent on site of present day Colston Hall
4 Orb and sceptre
5 15th century
6 Chancery, Bristol Mercantile, Family, County Courts
7 St John the Baptist
8 1692
9 Red
10 c.1456
11 Thomas Clarkson ▶ To research into the condition of slaves
12 The Unknown Deep
13 Ich Dien ▶ One and all
14 Haren/Ems ▶ Two
15 40 The Grove ▶ 30 ▶ Five
16 Fairhaven ▶ A pottery
17 930
18 Prince George of Denmark, consort to Queen Anne

WALK 4
CASTLE PARK

1 Because it enters Queen Square at the mid-point of one of the sides
2 Ship, Port, Fish
3 The Chapel of St Clement
4 Sailors
5 1699
6 Bristol Free Library
7 1673
8 1744 ▶ William Halfpenny
9 Burton
10 The Merchant Navy
11 A bomb in 1941
12 It has a second hand
13 Georges and Co. Ltd
14 Four
15 Because evidence was found in his waste – 'peafowl, pheasant and partridge bones' ▶ A hidden tunnel
16 The Normandy Landings of the Second World War
17 Kate Malone in 1993 ▶ The pupils of Brimsham Green School
18 Newgate jail
19 Robert Southey, who lived 1774–1843
20 Joseph Cottle 1770–1853
21 John Cabot
22 Market Chambers
23 The letter A
24 Exchange Buildings
25 Justice and Enterprise
26 1714

WALK 5
THE UNDERFALL

1 A castle
2 Building 30 Bristol Docks
3 Fishing
4 'Encouragement'
5 Two dogs
6 Chris Baldwin
7 Chatterton, Tyndall, Cary Grant and William Penn
8 Great Western Dockyard ▶ Six
9 50 years ▶ Royal Naval Volunteer Reserve
10 Poole's Wharf
11 Two
12 1831
13 Four
14 Flat-sided (or octagonal)
15 Choose from: provides air ventilation; allows longer working in winter; materials need not be carried far
16 R.B. Boatbuilding Ltd
17 *Albion* ▶ Harbourmaster's office hours: Mon–Thurs 8.00–5.00; Friday 8.00–4.30; outside normal hours: evenings until one hour after sunset.
18 1804–09
19 Ships
20 1986
21 'through the city'
22 Bristol Marina Office
23 Bristol Old Vic's scenic workshop
24 Smit International ▶ A gantry crane
25 Aardman
26 Ashley Down Junior School, Bishopsworh C of E Junior School, Teyfant Community School, Holy Cross Catholic Primary School and Hillcrest Primary School
27 *Tower Belle*
28 Three alder trees ▶ Stothert and Pitt ▶ 1973 ▶ Miranda Guinness
29 Tea sweetened with sugar
30 *Mayflower* ▶ 1973 ▶ Charles Hill
31 Electricity
32 The enslavement and exploitation of countless African men, women and children
33 Bristol International Youth Hostel

WALK 6
CHRISTMAS STEPS

1 Trade
2 Singing
3 D
4 A sailing ship/*The Matthew*
5 Bordeaux Quay (Bordeaux is Bristol's twin city in France)
6 A warrior
7 1983
8 Seven ▶ Wrestling, music and dance
9 Two
10 1483
11 Gryphons
12 Spiral
13 To have a rest!
14 1669 ▶ Six
15 The Three Sugar Loaves
16 St Bartholomews
17 Nothing – sorry, trick question
18 A medieval fireplace
19 The Crown Court
20 He was Mayor of Bristol in 1481
21 The Guildhall
22 11 minutes
23 'This is the gift of George White of Bristol, merchant brother unto Dr Thomas White a famous benefactor of this city AD 1631'
24 Animals
25 A long beard
26 King George V
27 Farming and mining
28 4 including Sabrina
29 Two hooks for hoisting
30 They are counterweights to enable the middle section of the bridge to be raised

WALK 7
LEWINS MEAD

1 St Mary-on-the-Quay
2 Archer Shee
3 Sugar cutters and sugar loaf
4 St Bartholomews
5 1240 ▶ Bristol Grammar School 1532–1767 ▶ Queen Elizabeth's Hospital School 1767–1847
6 A sugar house ▶ 352 (we think!)
7 MP for the city 1868–85
8 Francesco, young knight of Assisi; kissing hand of leper; A fair bride, poverty; renounces worldly possessions; Francis takes Clare into the order; Francis tames the wolf of Agobro ▶ 1250 ▶ 1538
9 John, Martha Maria, Susannah, Selina and John James
10 1672
11 The centuries
12 10
13 1500
14 It is the only municipally owned church in the country ▶ St Marks
15 Hannover (1947), Bordeaux (1947), Porto (1984), Tblisi (1988) and Beira (1990) ▶ A scroll
16 Abbey Church of St Augustine ▶ The Chapter House
17 Bristol Cathedral School

WALK 8
ST MICHAEL'S HILL

1 Friendly Society, Bridge Castle
2 The ceramics in the windows show:
   tobacco, wool, wine and leather and
   chocolate (in Host Street)
3 Zerodegrees is a microbrewery and
   restaurant
4 Griffen Court. The White Lodge sign gives
   a date of 1413
5 15 separate panes make up each window
6 King David
7 Micawber's/The Scotchman and his Pack
8 A bell
9 Eight
10 St Michael's Parish Hall
11 5266
12 Possibly to stop carriages getting too close
   to the house walls and demolishing them!
13 They are not straight / level
14 BBC Radio Bristol ▶ Bristol ▶ 15 October
   1932 (Cabot Trail) ▶ 1948 (centenary of
   ownership) ▶ Nova Scotia (Canadian
   Province)